While Waiting

The Musings of a Complicated Mailman

LaGuan Rodgers

Fulton Books, Inc.
Meadville, PA

Published by Fulton Books 2020

ISBN 978-1-64654-278-9 (paperback)
ISBN 978-1-64654-279-6 (digital)

Printed in the United States of America

For any of those who get up in the morning and decide to try.

—*LR*

These are just some of the many things I've
thought about while waiting...

WHILE WAITING

I never liked when my stepfather would drive me to school. It wasn't because I was embarrassed by his car; the '87 Pontiac got us where we needed to be and then some. It was more so how I found him to be weak. He let my mom rule him, and somehow, I thought his frayed machismo might find my skin like a plotting ointment. I found myself studying the sky for planes from that back seat window, most of all trying to guess exactly where a given hunk of traveling metal and its passengers were off to. I'm pretty sure my guesses were always confined to the states, as the geography of thinking beyond and what places fit where would get lost just around the time Sean's car would halt and I'd shuffle to homeroom.

"Can I get you anything else, maestro?" my waiter asks.

For the past twenty minutes or so, I've been slowly sipping a black coffee and picking at this dry blueberry muffin, waiting for Gianna to arrive. I'm not buying anything else. She is lucky I agreed to come to this damn diner. The parking is so-so, and some of our most memorable arguments happened in the booths here. Whoever made the menu goes skimp on the omelet, and there's something I don't trust about their maple syrup, like a station with gas prices lower than nearby spots.

"Thanks, buddy, but no, I'm okay," I reply.

The waiter has pillows under his eyes, not the glaring hangover or midterm-up-all-night weights, but somewhat noticeable, especially by another night owl. He has yet to declare his name, and I haven't cared to ask. I study his veiny hands, and though his short fingernails are without dirt, I suspect he still lets a family member cut his hair. And who the hell is maestro anyway? I put my head down to tear at the muffin and shift my cup, yet he stays in the same spot. I'm hoping it doesn't come to the inevitable: the stage where I have to get in his tired face and let him know I'm not with that sugary stuff.

"Their uniforms do nothing for me," he says.

"I'm sorry. What?" I ask.

"The Trail Blazers' uniforms," he answers, pointing up to the flat screen positioned in the corner. A replay of last night's game versus Oklahoma City is playing with the volume off. "Red and black work together, but ugh, they can do better with those bending lines that take up most of the jersey. It's all too…too…too…I don't know, but once I think of something better, I should reach out to their people."

Gianna told me the owner of Swan Street is originally from Portland, and the dude has yet to come to grips he is more than 2,600 miles from home. The pennants and postcards on the wall scream of everything Oregon and his Left Coast Is the Best Coast pie is a hit here in WNY. She made me try it the night we first hooked up. I didn't like it, but I said I did.

"I'm a fashion student at Buff State," the waiter points out.

"Oh, wow, that's what's up" is my reply. I give him a look as if to ask why isn't he serving other people, yet it's midmorning and empty, and the rush from the Larkin Building across the street won't come about until lunch hour.

"Where do you go?"

"Oh, I'm not in school right now."

"Guy, I feel you. It's not for everybody. When you think about it, they're just teaching us how to make someone else money. Fashion is the closest thing to independence if you ask me. But I hear there's a big need for the trades nowadays because all of the dinosaurs our grandparents used to call in the Yellow Pages are retiring, and few young folks are stepping into those jobs, you know."

"Good point," I say with a shrug.

I forgot to put on my Timex, so I'm starting to stare at the spot where the tan line on my wrist will eventually be. Doing odd landscaping gigs two or three times a week every summer will do that. Gianna has been sending me e-mails of jobs here and there. I've filled out a few applications online, yet there's something discouraging about completing questionnaires where you can't tell the truth.

Where the hell is she? For the past six months, we've been doing the distance thing after she moved to Albany for some job in a big library. I can't remember all the details, but she's happy and spends less time knitting uneven sweaters for her yorkie and sending me recipes off Pinterest she knows I'll never make on my own. Today is supposed to be the day we decide.

"Coming!" the waiter whose name is Jackson shouts. I now know this little useless tidbit because a male voice from the kitchen yelled his name while I was staring out the window. Three tulips stand at attention from the flower bed that needs just as much attention as the blueberry muffin ingredients. She must think I have all day.

The entrance door swings open. A toddler boy wearing overalls wobbles over the threshold. His mouth already has stains of juice, and he wants no assistance from his parents who give off this que será, será vibe. The man and woman scan the room and locate me in their tripod scope of discovery, only to flash grins at me before muttering some baby gibberish to the little one, as he has already rung the front counter bell enough to awaken something in the basement of a day failing to officially start.

"Hey, fine folks, how are you?" Jackson asks the newest patrons, sort of doing some half-hearted skip to the front. "As you can see, we are jam-packed, but I'm sure we can find something cozy and comfortable for ya." Everybody laughs, except the tike and I.

"Oh no…no…no, Brady," the mother says, smiling once she realizes her little person is running toward my booth.

She is too late. He grabs the second menu from the table and waves it wildly like my grandmother sometimes does with those usher-appointed fans during stuffy marathon church services.

"You eat" is what I make out from the boy. "Him eat, right?"

"I'm so sorry," the mother says. "He's a traveler."

I look at the father who just shakes his head, as if there is more he wishes he could tell me over a Cuban and some bourbon.

By now, the mother has come over to my booth and ushers away her little explorer by the arm.

"Him eat, right?" continues the boy. "Him do it…"

"Yes, honey," says his mom. "Go to daddy."

"This is why I hate going too many places in a day," the father says in a tone somewhere between madness and unbridled surrender.

"It's fine," the mother says. "It really is okay."

"Well, let's get you guys seated," Jackson breaks in, mustering up a manufactured smile he's most likely perfected in the back kitchen or voguing outside one of his textile classes.

I look at the clock on the wall behind the front counter and spread some butter on the muffin.

*****

When Gianna moved into her upstairs apartment on Claremont Avenue with her two girlfriends, I helped them. Being her boyfriend, I knew such heavier things would fall to me. We found a way to defy trigonometry, stubbornly bending half-painted corners with used furniture and appliances. She is the organized type of XX, and that day, the Eisenhower in her began to bloom.

She elected to drive the U-Haul with Jamie and Allison, as I was content to drive my own car and meet them at the new place. My commander of a woman backed the truck on to the lawn, got out, and handed her troupe the instructions and goals written on loose-leaf. I put the paper in my back pocket and just grabbed labeled boxes. The first few trips, I placed them where they needed to be; the carefully taped cardboard containing shampoo, tampons, and razors found their home in the bathroom. Maybe it was because no one else's boyfriends showed up until I was a sweat-stained version of former self, or the way Gianna stood in the downstairs doorway with frustration when her foolproof battle maps left no margin for things falling apart, or how the summer rain would slap our efforts then backpedal into some distant pocket on the other side of town before I could adequately curse it, but I found myself unashamedly putting boxes in rooms where they didn't belong.

We later ate pizza and drank bottled water on the floor, a collegiate picnic of sorts. Both boyfriends, whose names I dismissed, looked as if they struggled to please any woman, and their talk of IPAs and invites to join a softball league only made my decision to leave more justifiable.

"Oh, before you go, lover, can you help me hang these?" Gianna asked me as she opened a box marked CLOCKS in black Sharpie. It wasn't her handwriting, and as she and I went room to room hanging ticking numbers with power drill and the dull need to be alone, the thought of that stayed long after I left.

*****

"Hey, Ian," Gianna says. She leans over and kisses both of my cheeks before sitting down.

"When did you come in? I didn't even see you."

"I'm a love ninja," she declares. "I move in silence."

"Well, Ms. Storm Shadow, are you having your usual? There's a new waiter working, and he is full of life."

"Be nice, lover."

"What makes you think I'm not."

"I know you."

"Do you, really?"

"I'd like to think I know if the man I love is being an asshole or not."

I still hear the ongoing jabber of my toddler friend from the other side of the diner, and once Jackson discovers I am no longer solo, he darts toward the action.

"You didn't tell me you were waiting on a lovely guest, my guy," Jackson shrieks. "Exciting."

"Good morning," Gianna says. "Is it still morning? No... wait...it's technically morning? Sorry my brain is in every county of the state today."

"No worries, I understand," Jackson replies. "It's finals time, and I'm the same way. I'm living the dream, though. Stress and all."

"If it isn't too much trouble, I think I'll try something new today."

"You have to get our new red velvet pancakes," our waiter urges. "To die for!"

"Hmmm, should I?" She calls my name, but I'm staring at little Brady who is biting his straw and too curious to be held at bay by whatever routine conversation his parents may be conducting.

"Ian?"

"What's up, GiGi?" I snap back onstage, knowing the second time she calls me is the important one of the two. I shrug and simply say it's spring.

"I am a horrible server," Jackson says. "I didn't start by asking you what you wanted to drink. I'm so caught up in the vibe of you two chirping birds."

Gianna orders the pancakes and asks for orange juice to come when the food arrives.

"Are we going to do this?" she asks.

"I'm prepared either way," I say.

"That's not the right answer. It's been three months."

"But how are you feeling?" I ask, picking out blueberries I can find in the torn pieces of muffin.

"Okay, I guess," she says. "I still get sick, and the new clothes fit now."

I want to bring up something about how I've applied to the latest jobs she's sent me, but I close my eyes and try to take it in every molecule of air in the building.

"What time do you have to be back tonight?" I ask.

"I don't. I already called in sick for tomorrow."

"Go easy. You're going to need those days later down the road."

"So you're saying you do want this, right?"

"I want to keep you happy and occupied."

I turn at the waist and find the tulips outside the window. I wish I could pick all three and the curtain would close.

"And here you go," Jackson declares with a smile, waiting for immediate approval. "I present delicious pancakes, your juice and our in-house maple syrup."

"It looks amazing," Gianna says.

"Is there anything else I can get you?" It's as if Jackson wishes he were the stack of crimson flapjacks with a melting cube of butter atop.

"We've got all the bases covered for now," she says. With fork and knife in hand, the woman I met at a farmer's market four summers ago puts a piece of pancake to my mouth. I submit to her honor and chew slowly so I can really give her the truth of it all.

"What do you think?"

"They're actually really good," I admit.

She takes a bite, and her eyes become big with unexpected glee.

"Boy, you better get one more taste because I can't promise I'll save anything else."

"Go ahead," I say. "It's all you. You need it for strength. After all…you know…"

"You act like it's some sort of plague, Ian."

"No, I don't. It's just…"

"It's just what?"

"A lot."

"No shit, man," she says, now with a tear bubbling at the corner of her eye nearest the window.

"We can make it work."

"Do you really want it to?"

"I'm here."

"Have you even thought of names?"

"Of course, I have." Really I haven't, and now would be a fantastic time for Jackson to save the scene.

"Have you told your mom?" she asks, still eating.

"Yeah, she knows."

"What are her thoughts?"

"You know my mom, GiGi."

"I don't want to play games."

"I see no ball or joystick."

"Answer a question for once in your life!" she shouts.

By now, the tears have bullied the break wall and run southward to a place I have little to no access to. It's one of those classic embarrassing moments when I sense all eyes are upon us, yet I have no hard evidence to support it other than the intuition that comes from past battlefields still ripe with blood. The Larkin Building traffic infiltrates what was an empty place of business.

"My mother told me to be a man," I say.

Gianna stares at me for a while before she finishes the plate of pancakes, only leaving streaks of red mingled with the sappy sauce that is the Oregonian's special recipe. Without as much time to devote to us any longer, our waiter gives me the check and says he hopes to see us soon. I tell him thank you and good luck with his exams before I make my way to the front counter where there is now a female waitress at the register.

"It seems you made a friend," Brady's mom says. "He hasn't stopped talking about the man who eats by himself." The family of three prepares to leave the diner, a precautionary measure on the part of the husband and father who doesn't want to cause a scene I suspect.

"Maybe I'll see you in this joint sometime soon, little man," I say to Brady. "Be good for your mommy and daddy."

I foot the bill and tip and wait for Gianna to come from the bathroom. I know she will want to take a walk and possibly talk more on what is a pleasant afternoon in early May. Once again, I'm looking out the window where I see Brady and his parents walking to their car. The father has little patience, and if it wasn't for his wife, who knows where that car would go? She is the reason her child gets away with picking one of the tulips I've been staring at all morning. That little boy doesn't have to take unnecessary long walks. If anything, I am sure he fixates on passing airplanes.

THE END

BASIC DOPAMINE

I feel orange embers gossiping on my scalp.
I feel hopeful.
I feel given up on.
I feel like I truly am worthy of a second act.
I feel enraged with myself.
I feel there is more to it all, and I am not permitted to proofread it.
I feel blindsided.
I feel easily discarded.
I feel forgotten about—the bull's eye of this new dementia.
I feel as though winter will be my dandiest season.
I feel full of effort—my endurance is thick.
I feel anxious for being mad because any comeback is justified.
I am tempted not to respond.
Voices make me feel.
Tomorrow is _____.

ROY G BIV

It's only fitting that colors evoke emotions. Right now, my favorite color is red. The deep brand. Red is for honest blood, the blood I'd give for those who've shockingly turned their backs on me. This is taking place all under a blue sky no less.

GROUNDED

The worst part of this punishment is not you making me stand one-inch away from the wall while facing it. It's the realization that the wall is actually a mirror and that you have yet to leave my side. Oh, and all the lights are on…

PRETTY'S CORNER

As they sat at their leaning table in the kitchen, Jodi wondered why her husband ate his cereal in such a way. He did the grocery shopping sure enough, so the sugary brands were okay, she thought, yet Shane never could leave it there. In the beginning, there was something she liked about his bony hands, but that morning, she focused on the long fingers wet at the tips—they sifted through to find just the marshmallows within the pink ocean of skim.

"Today would be a good day to go, you know," Jodi said, feeling hopeful.

"Go where?" Shane replied. His voice was somewhere in the deep, buried between rocks and worn-out lullabies. He kept his head down and fiddled through the bowl until he pinched two pieces.

"I mean it's a perfect day for it," Jodi said. "It's crisp, but not too cold. They may even have the giraffes out. You know how much Micah—"

Outside, the garbage and recycling cans sat jostled up against the curb. Shane's cousin, Marc, worked for the mayor's impact team and fetched their raked leaves, that is, if they only used the clear bags. He hadn't come. Yet.

"Are we doing this today?" asked Shane. The man whose wife once thought he possessed the mitts of a pianist going places, stood up and wiped his hands over his back pockets and tossed the plastic bowl in the sink, which had no other dishes.

"Do you still…" Jodi nodded toward Shane's left pocket which contained his wallet of mostly business cards crumpled at the edges, a few coupons, and a renewed driver's license. His carabiner, which contained more comic hero trinkets than keys, stayed attached to his belt loop along with the wooden bottle opener reserved for Deckers.

"Jodi, please."

"Don't, babe. I still carry mine," she said as she quickly reached for her mint purse on the side of her chair and snatched out her pocketbook. To Shane's relief, she just patted the wallet and didn't unfasten the clasp unlike so many times before, especially on nights when the dark felt blacker and he returned. "Things are getting better."

"For who?" Shane mumbled. He cleared his throat and faced the window as each hand gripped opposite ends of the sink. "Listen, we're down to one banana and the store has bone-in chops for sale. Where's the list? I'll get what we need."

"I'm low on hazelnut creamer," Jodi answered. "We're good on frozen veggies and the plain rolls you like. But Pretty needs some tending."

"Sheesh, I just got food for her last week," Shane stated, obviously annoyed.

Jodi usually gauged her husband's anger by looking at the tips of his ears. If they reddened like spilled cranberries over snow, things got heavier. This time, she didn't care if he was or not.

"Get the pellets this time, please, instead of the flakes," Jodi made her voice go up into the high realm of elflike octaves, a plea for a truce in her universe. "I've been finding her digestion is better with those. Who would've thought?"

"The car has gas, right?" Shane asked.

If it didn't, it was his doing, Jodi thought. Her hands were still shaky, and when she drove, it was only to see her dad and sister fifteen minutes away on the West Seneca border. They'd do black coffee, talk about the custom planner business she put on hiatus, she'd cry, hug them both too roughly, and drive home. The vibrations of the steering wheel took residency in her palms and wrists and usually stayed there until it was feeding time. Shane was good about massaging the shakes at first, but lately, it was her, some rubber band exercises she googled, and ice in a sandwich baggie whenever she remembered to put it back in the freezer.

"You know I don't let it go under a quarter, babe," Jodi said. "I got you." She made a kissing sound in his direction. "Don't forget to—"

He came over to her. She hugged him like a grizzly. There was his normal peck on her forehead then he walked to the side door. The Volkswagen started up, and though she often tried without looking out the window, she couldn't hear him backing out the driveway. In the linen closet between the master bedroom and bathroom was the vacuum. She unraveled the chord and went into their son's room.

*****

They stayed local after Shane found a position at the university to teach barely twentysomethings and nontraditionals civil engineering three weekdays and Saturdays. It gave Jodi time for her target audience who wanted cute pastel stickers, foldout pages, and risky fonts for their busy planners. Her husband respected the craft, yet sometimes joked about how she went to great lengths and burned through a lot of precious time to make things for strangers who, in the end, would just spill lattes and oolong on her life's work.

One Saturday in March, two years ago, she and the three-year-old left the house in the blue Dodge Caliber for the craft store. She buckled him into the front-facing car seat and checked it twice. *He's in tight. The chicken is thawing in the sink. Don't forget the chalkboard pencils toward the back when we get there*, she thought. She went through a drive-through without barely any holdup—a coffee with one sugar and two creams for her and a chocolate ring donut for Micah whose royal knit hat swallowed up his curly hair to the point that all she could remember was the light snow and the chunkiness of his cold cheeks.

The light turned green, and the last thing she saw was the few snowflakes that descended on her window like paratroopers only to land softly then disappear. By the time Shane got there, the police and responders had been there for some time. They blocked everything from the corners off. Jodi wouldn't let go of the wheel or turn to see what the back looked like. He was gone on impact, a day drunk with warrants who ignored a red. Jodi wondered if his hands ever felt the same vibrations.

Things sort of settled, and eventually Jodi started to see someone. Shane's insurance paid most of it, and the bus got her to appointments. Her psychologist—a young Indian man with muscular arms and a bit of a stomach—would offer gum before the Friday sessions started. On days when she felt like talking, she declined the offer. The other days, she just sat and listened to the music of her own chewing as the man filled the room with lost attempts. She had trouble with his last name, so she asked to use his first name, an honest request he was fine with.

Arjun's office gave off a cozy feel with its carpet and mid-century modern armchair. A fiddle-leaf fig plant sat in the window, and a framed poster of national parks badges hung above his desk, which he rarely sat at. Shane referred to the man as Jodi's helper and blamed him for the addition, for it happened to be a Friday when his wife came home with a pale-blue plastic bag filled with water and gallon-sized glass bowl in hand, all for a goldfish he was told to call Pretty.

Inside the room, everything was kept just how it was the day it all occurred. Jodi would open the door gradually as if it was seven in the morning and the space still contained a sleeping child. The bookcase housed stuffed animals in its corners, and folded blankets were laid at the foot of the twin. The sheets and pillowcases matched—a vintage print of floating balloons and waiting carousels. Small slippers sat by the nightstand, and the white rocking chair Shane built himself to read stories and rock back and forth wildly during playtime once in a while after papers were graded only moved when bumped by the vacuum's bulky body.

An effort to use the room for any sort of storage on Shane's end resulted in the heavier things. The Indian culprit welcomed group sessions. The following Fridays, he'd only be met by his imperiled female. Pretty's glass domain made its way from Jodi's craft room to a sunlit spot in the living room atop a square oak table. The bowl left the house, and the orange little dart of spawns now had a tank with bubbling filter and coral green rocks to circumnavigate. "They tell us to give her pad a good shine every seven to ten days, lover," Jodi would say to her husband. "But to be on the proper side, let's clean it an extra day. She really does deserve it all." Shane handed over the tools like scalpels and tin pans during surgery and followed every bubble he could from the time it left the filter and popped at the surface.

*****

The door opened, and Shane carried the bag loosely in the cuff of his arm. Maneuvers like that were unnecessary, Jodi thought.

"It was a zoo..." The faux pianist-turned-carpenter on sabbatical paused before he stepped on the scale. "Better yet, a madhouse down there. Everybody had to be thinking the same damn thing. I got the chops and a mix of green and ready-to-go bananas. If they get spotty, we can throw them in smoothies or whatever."

"Or some banana bread?"

"You haven't made a loaf in ages." He wanted to say more. He looked over her and fiddled with the bottle opener on his keychain. It was her job to put away the items.

"I thawed the ground lamb. I figured it would go good with green beans and the yams in the back of the fridge," Jodi came back. "You have to remember not to put them so far back so ice doesn't get on them. You know it still does that, and we don't have it on a very cold setting."

"Nothing an oven can't solve at four-hundred twenty-five degrees," he said and turned his hollow hands and shrugged his shoulders.

"Did you stop by the pet store and get the pellets?" Jodi asked half excited, half preparatory.

Shane motioned over to the countertop and began to walk toward the living room with plans for the TV. "Yeah, it's in there. They asked if I wanted a bag, but I just put in the reusable tote I use. That store isn't on the way home, you know."

Jodi held the bag by one strap and put her other hand inside as if she picked a folded sheet of paper out of a magician's hat at a child's party. Somehow, she grabbed the side of the can which did not declare the contents, yet she felt off. She turned the can and made her way over to the aquarium.

"These are flakes," she said. Her voice returned to the underground pitch it had so many Mondays when it was hard to put toes to the carpet and jobs like mustering the oomph to pee seemed congratulatory.

"Oh, they didn't have the pellets," said her husband who pressed the remote just as fast as he used to write percentages in red ink on exams. "It doesn't matter. It's all food in the end."

"I asked you for pellets!" Jodi screamed. "I know you didn't look or ask anybody. I know it."

Her words met her male detractor's force field and bounced off unclaimed. She snatched the remote from his tentacles and got into his chest.

"What's your problem!" Shane shouted. He stalked his way over to Pretty's wet world and began to bang the fish's food on the oak table uncontrollably. "I looked. They didn't have it. I brought back something for your swimming Jesus. Make it work. I came back with—"

"You're hurting Pretty. You're hurting Pretty. Damn it, Shane. That's too much vibration. Just be gentler, you beast." Her words echoed through her own hands, and the wettest tears replaced the snowflakes.

"How do you even know if that damn thing is even a girl? It could be a boy, you know. A boy…a swimming boy…"

"You think I'm crazy, don't you?" Jodi asked, both knees stapled to the hardwood floor, strands of hair stuck to her cheek where the flakes should've rightfully melted. "I'll show you, babe." She burst into laughter and made her way off the floor and adjusted the bra strap back onto her shoulder.

"Jodi, come on," Shane said. His ears were red by the lobes, and once again, he fidgeted with the bottle opener. He'd been here just as much as Arjun's client had. "I'm going up the way. I'll be back."

"He never got to eat his donut, Shane," Jodi admitted. "Still in the bag. He was taking it out."

Nothing but the sound of the fish tank's filter tested the space.

He started the car and drove away. For the first time, she could hear some faint squealing of brakes as the car backed out and drove past her bus stop at the corner. It was the evening, and by that time, the stars shined across the October sheet like pins on the chest of a revived general. She cut off the TV and looked out the front window until she remembered the lamb. She put on her apron and took out a plate from the cupboard to mold the meat into patties.

The doorbell rang. She hoped Shane was locked in tightly on a stool at Decker's. Hard knocks fell on the side door of the house. She wiped her hands on her thighs and opened the door with torque.

"Hello, who is it?" she said before the main and screen doors separated.

It was Marc, in his reflective jacket and muddy boots.

"Oh hey, Marc. You're out kind of late."

Marc pushed his hat up around his hairline and scratched his forehead. "Hey, I noticed you guys never brought your cans in. Heading back to the yard. We had some guys break down a few streets over, so I'll take the overtime, what the hell."

"Oh geez, thanks," Jodi said. "Where would we be without you?"

"You got any for me this week?"

"Oh yeah, I almost forgot that too." Her voice softened and went into a lighter cave. "There, by the fence. We'll have them by the curb next time. Sorry."

It was then when Jodi realized the two piles of leaves that sat in black bags. Shane claimed the store didn't have any when he restocked. She waited for Marc to notice the infraction.

"I apologize for the leaves being in the wrong bags, kind sir." She felt the need to face it head-on.

"Oh, it's no biggie," said Shane's cousin. "I'll take them for you, but only this time. City rules, you feel me?" He let out a chuckle and wagged his index finger, playfully.

"Gotcha."

"Say, where's he anyway?"

"Oh, Shane?" Jodi asked, yet already ahead of the curve. "You know him. He's out taking on the world, doing his thing."

Marc carried the two heavy bags in one trip. Jodi wondered if his hands ever felt vibrations from that kind of work. The white pickup drove away, and she stayed at the edge of the driveway until the orange flashing lights faded under the trees as if the night was a pencil with its own eraser. She went inside and turned an aisle on the stove top. But before that, she flipped on the side light for Shane. He'd come home at some point.

THE END

When we hear someone utter the famous words "I love you," I can't help but wonder what the fine print reads. Often our "love" comes with clauses and rigid stipulations. The more honest way to put it is "I love you if you continue to do this…" or "I love you so as long as you don't do that…" For one to gently brush the twitching hand of a lover and whisper "I love you, but I'm not in love with you" is to say the unloved still possesses all the same ingredients for a tasty dish, yet the victor's palette has changed and no longer wishes to sit at the table; despite all the beverages available, they can't wash away the bad taste. The term *unconditional love* still conjures up anxiety in the still of a winter evening. To love is to stay with another misfit well into the night and within the infancy of the morning. He or she who has nothing to gain yet something of value to squander shrugs and says "Let's try again. The sun is out."

Some days you just need to hear everything will be okay from someone or something or somewhere you come across, and even if it's only
for a skinny millisecond, you believe them.

There's something I find very sad and yet wondrous about libraries. To me, a good book is to be owned, if possible. I have to touch it, look deep into its cover, write in its margins and tight spaces. Ultimately, I want to travel back to it like the lighthouses of someone's youth when some force in life pushes me in its direction for whatever benefit it offers me. I don't want to be left in awe and then be told the pleasure is borrowed or rented. An essential book is like a close friend who you don't talk with often, yet when you encounter him or her at a table or under a dying tree, it's as if the world makes a little more sense.

FAREWELL TO DIPLOMACY

I wanted to know the real you, so I conceived this rudimentary idea and let it hatch: I made you mad.

MY TRUE LOVE

I'll probably meet you in the peanut butter aisle at the store, or
as we both scramble to make the door of the bank at 4:59 on a Friday.
I'll insist you go ahead of me,
yet the way you'll say "No, it's okay…"
will rattle around in your jaw, owning the air and its woven particles.
The annoyed teller will barely make eye contact.
I'll be on my way.
Then as I drop my receipt, which falls at your salt-stained boot,
you'll look at it and shrug.
"I understand," you'll say.
Somehow, I'll just know, and the skirmishes within will subside
until lapels seek ornaments.

UNTITLED
(BEFORE BREAKFAST)

Yesterday is gone.
                    Today has a heartbeat.

TARA

I've read your text messages,
and seen you in unfiltered photos.
The red of your lips copying and pasting
a bent smile from forest to Ferris wheel along the floating metropolis.
I still haven't heard your voice.
I want to hear it,
and how it will mispronounce my name.
If I do, maybe…just maybe, it will replace the spooky ones waltzing
in my head.

True courage is the ability to do what's right when it's least conve-
nient. It's essentially affixing one's heart to the North Star despite the
most daunting of overcasts.

For many of us who have trouble falling asleep and fight far too many bouts with insomnia, it's not a matter of us attempting to extend the present day, but it's more of the fear of the next day's beginning and what goblins await to take the place of alarm clocks. Is there something out there that tells the morning it is genuinely needed, and how much is being dependent upon a new day feeling good about its own self?

It's those subjects and ideas that won't leave our brains that we need to write about the most, whether it's within the creative realm or the burning need to declare a cause connected to the empowerment and enrichment of humanity. If we both submit to and cultivate these visions, which pleasantly pester the live wires in our minds, there is no telling where the page and chisel can take us. These stories keep staring at the ceiling at night while the sound of rain-slick tires and distant horns speak their own languages outside our apartment windows. They cause us to catch ourselves daydreaming, both palms cupping our chin, only to be interrupted by the ringing of an office phone. Our worlds will only continue to lack harmony until we set out on a quest to see sounds and speak colors. The anecdotes that won't leave us must be entertained and developed! What could be of more importance?

Fall in love with books. People change. Books do not.

U-HAULS

Moving on and moving out are two entirely different dances yet fraternal on the surface. One requires relentless effort. The other is the gradual maturation of whispers coursing through the veins until the heart is bold enough to beat to a new rhythm. I have to admit. I do not know which is which.

With the exception of watching a loved one wither away, the saddest scenes in life are when close companions become strangers. The magnetism dissolves. Though one swears by the heavens he will always be there for the other, there comes a distinct moment in time when both parties realize nothing will be as it once was. What used to be long meaty conversations on the sunken couch will be replaced by clipped small talk when they happen to stroll upon each other during the holiday hustle and Saturday markets, if they even choose to acknowledge friendly ghosts. Kisses become half-hearted handshakes and surgical hugs. It will be hard to recall how she used to ever feel incomplete in her lover's absence in a city that is wide and full of dreams to do more…to become more…while sinking less and taking priority over any teenage pinky promise and out-of-order gumball machine.

There comes a time throughout each day when we are justified for being full of ourselves. After all, there are so many things, purposely and unintentionally, trying to empty us.

Realistically, in a given situation, we may come away with more questions unanswered, much to our mental state's chagrin and torture. It's like the corner pieces to a puzzle blowing over a dissolving cliff before the hand can snatch them from the swirling wind. However, it's up to us to accept the concrete facts and process the story wherever it ended, albeit sour or incomplete. Of course, such sobering realization requires the "T-word." We know the one…that T-word…that keeps clocks of all kinds in business.

If we can muster up enough courage and humility to ask a sincere question, we might just be better for it.

True living is coming across the simple and stopping long enough to soak it all in. It's sending a postcard to someone who doesn't know you're on an adventure. It's stomping through rain puddles on the street you grew up on. It's the look of a little one when he or she first sees their cold breath in winter. It's the smell of golden flapjacks bombarding your nose on a Saturday morning.

Living is going to a movie by yourself and not feeling insecure. It's sitting on a pastel bench and watching cars go by as they rattle over potholes. It's reading the liner notes to a favorite album. It's wearing the sweater that should've been thrown away years ago and gripping a warm cup of tea by the window.

Living is handling a kite and purposely letting go of it just to see it disappear into the horizon. It's daydreaming on your back in the grass, oblivious to time. It's electing to ride in the back seat, studying other travelers' license plates. It's placing a dream on the moon's surface and revisiting it every night before slumber calls you by your middle name.

Living is listening to the story when our grandparents fell in love. It's tossing autumn leaves high into the sky. It's window-shopping in an assuming little town found by accident.

Living is to see the cardinal and blue jay land at the same hanging feeder, yet there is harmony in the quest for food. It's dancing off-rhythm, not giving a damn who giggles. It's saying "I love you" to that which owns deaf ears.

Most of all, real living just wants to be. The texture. The pace. The predicate of the day.

Young children tend to think of a parent as a superhero of sorts, not knowing the full extent of "big people" flaws. Within their bright irises, little sons and daughters see no wrong in mom and dad. Perhaps it's when kids begin to see themselves in their authority figures when the shift takes place. The lad who lacks patience was given up on at some point. The young lady who is hyper-judgmental was first judged harshly by someone close.

It's imperative that families maintain evolving levels of transparency for the overall emotional and social vitality of its members. Not only will occasions for acceptance to blossom be more probable, but there could also be long-lasting breakthroughs in the name of solid bonds. In the end, the younger crowd might just thank the grayer generation for not having it all together and vice versa.

I'm still foolish enough to believe each human deserves something delicious to put in his or her belly, a love that lasts at least through the changing of four seasons, and an unrestricted view of the immense stars without disturbance.

FRED AKA FREDONIA
AKA OUR 1ST TIME

The late September air won't leave my skin,
I rewind, pause, and zoom in on the crunchiness of your tan boots
over campus leaves.
Even the maples stood at attention and stepped aside,
as you led the way like a proven chaperone.
An evening for omnivores,
hungry yet full,
curious without anxiety,
gabbing just to fill the empty trail with words.
The trees purposely got out of our way,
all of them magistrate green,
flirting with orange and yellow possibilities.
Perhaps one tower of bark hinted I should turn around and come
home.
I didn't listen.
Now you're the ghost hovering over my night lamp.

One of the most beautiful things in life is you never know where inspiration will come from in a given day if you just open your eyes, speak to others, and listen to the world record itself.

Truth be told, we don't choose the great albums and books of our lives. They really choose us and grab hold of us wherever we are on our journeys, whether it's making a pleasurable experience that much more enjoyable, and later on, nostalgic or serving as the floating bridge between present heartache and deferred healing.

Attempting to accomplish something in the name of revenge or merely to prove someone wrong will only take us so far. Sooner or later, we will have to do it because the act moves us closer to being better versions of ourselves. That's if, in fact, there's a desire for any lasting effects. Isn't that what any sane person, full of flaws and a few bright edges, should strive for before closing the blinds at night?

My love for my mother has never changed. However, the level of respect has indeed grown over the years. Mostly because of what her existence symbolizes to me, seeing how I, too, am a parent now. The first adjective tapping on my mind when describing her is *selfless*. She is the embodiment of *others-before-I*, which lends itself to less opportunities for her own much-needed self-care and recharging. I can't ever think of a time when she's allowed herself to do a shabby job. Whether it's decking the halls with Christmas magic, hosting a memorable gathering, or cleaning a dust-plagued nook in the house, her diligence is an extension of her being. She wouldn't necessarily express it, but rest assured, if her signature is on something, whatever it is can be looked upon with certitude and as a job well done. With figures like *Ma* as an unwavering example, I want my name to be synonymous with the word *quality* when others look down the finite hallways of my time here.

Yes. We can learn a lot from people's words, but have we ever stopped to think about the things we learned from people's silence?

As I look back on my grandfather's life, I think I learned some lifelong lessons just by riding in the car with him as he would drive here and there. On cold nights, my grandfather would show up, a nub of cigar hanging from the corner of his mouth, outside a mall or movie theater when I'd call for somebody to take my friends and me home.

I can't recall him ever complaining, and he made sure everyone got home safely like it was his duty. On other occasions, I'd ride along with him during his days as a chauffeur, just so I could see different streets and soak up new sights and sounds from the passenger side window. My favorite part of these treks would be on the way home when we'd stop for food and listen to tunes on the radio.

Values like service, kindness, and dependability took solid shape as far as my mom's dad was concerned. Not one for the "wow, look at me" sensationalism, he wanted everybody who came into his circle to feel valued and cared for. Years later, as Alzheimer's steadily robbed him of might and memory, his voice could no longer be heard. It was during these times that I longed to talk to him most. However, I had a ton of great stories and solid lessons to draw from, courtesy of the patriarch whose quiet service spoke louder than a hundred amplified guitars.

EMPATHY

If you've never had to endure the presence of monsters in your room through the night, please be aware that these ghouls that lie between the mattress and the box spring are not always figments of others' imaginations. How frightening must it be to our friends when they'd rather stay in their rooms and battle identified beasts more so than face allies with shrinking eardrums and calcifying hearts who passively wait on the other side of the doorknob?

One day, whether it be a beautiful clear kind of day where the yellow sun hangs like a suspended yolk or one of those dreary nights when rain makes us less shallow, we will all be faced with the task of forgiving someone who will never forgive us. Somehow, a skeleton key will appear and gradually release our shackles, and the view from our bedroom windows won't ever be the same. As is the unfailing nature of the diamondback and his brethren, a dead skin will be lost for the better. Those once-tight lungs will adopt a new expansion and capacity to take in the smell of sea-foam rolling in. And maybe, just maybe, we will be comfortable playing the villain in someone else's traveling vaudeville where each violation has its own pen name. And so we bow…

There's something intrinsically calming deep down when you know you are doing your absolute best.

Competition essentially involves your best attempting to trump someone else's best at the most crucial of moments. But where did this need to show dominance over another come from exactly? It's on display within the animal world from Arctic wolf packs to domesticated dogs passing each other in a park. Furthermore, competition manifests escalating degrees—either reward or repercussion. On the sidewalk, the kid who wins a footrace is applauded. In sports, trophies and jewelry are dispensed to the victor(s). War is a sad feat where the objective is to eliminate one's "opponent" and lessen the probability of losers being afforded the chance to tell their own stories in history books.

Inasmuch as there are two sides to every story, there are two parts: the table of contents and the point at which we lower our voices.

When I find my children fighting over something silly or being clearly unkind to the other, I think about many of the serious battles awaiting them outside our door, which then leads me to ponder the state of so many fragmented households. Perhaps it can be categorized as righteous anger or passion bubbling over the rim, but I find myself—with my fist pounding whatever the nearest surface is—shouting to them, "Don't fight against each other! Fight for each other!" Imagine what this generation could accomplish if this were so?

SUICIDE

Before you take matters into your own aching hands,
just know there are princes and paupers,
who would kill for your life.
Come inside, and let's talk.

The person who folds the fitted sheet in the house really has the upper hand.

I had just about finished my workout one Sunday morning in the early fall when I came across a handsome man on the top step of the rear entrance to the Albright-Knox Art Gallery. With a face clean-shaven and decked in a navy-blue suit and tan shoes, the man appeared to be waiting for something or someone. I thought to myself, *It's not a day when folks typically get married but whatever.*

I made my way to my car, and shortly after, I saw a beaming young lady in a white lace dress who walked with a haste toward the columns of the gallery. I made a joke of how the groom was nervous about potentially being stood up and how she should hurry to relieve his stress. It wasn't hard to notice the happiness in the woman's face as she cut through the crisp September air on a mission. Minutes later, I saw the gentleman again, and coincidentally, his car was parked near mine. I couldn't help but tell him to cherish the blessing of finding a good woman and how he must try his best to honor her and do right through the years. "I most certainly intend to, sir," he said with a level of confidence and nervousness, which refreshed my soul and ultimate hope in love.

And just like that, the couple rode off, but before they did, the groom didn't forget to open the passenger side and help his queen get in, making sure she was totally secure, then he gently closed the door. I stood still and watched that car down the road until I could no longer see it.

Our imaginations flourish when we are either most bored or unsatisfied with our realities. However, the imagination is based on at least the tiniest confetti shreds of what already exists. In other words, make believe has two rightful parents: our past and our present.

GOD

I AM not the executive producer of evil.
I can be jealous—as for you, do not covet.
All these "how comes," "whys," and "are you up theres?" get on my
nerves.
Yes, I sanctioned the tsunami,
which erased monuments and schoolchildren,
yet love Me, damn it!
Wait…they say I'm slow to answer e-mails?
I take my own name in vain?
If you need Me,
I'll be sure to send my winged publicists.
I AM the hobo you ignored yesterday—
the indie artist who cannot curse in songs,
with an open tab and quiet office.
Unimpressed by those towering huts they call cathedrals—
the rec league is predictable, picking Me to play center.
I know you need Me,
I AM double-parked by the pyramids, knitting mercy.
Before I vanish,
I have a secret to tell:
I, and I alone, broke up The Beatles.

I'd encourage anyone to travel how they can and when they can and as far as they can. For to travel—in the physical sense—is to take in a new canvas while wearing the same pair of glasses. But what comes of traveling when we put on a new pair of eyewear? We don't necessarily have to be photographed at the base of the Eiffel Tower or rub our hands across the wood of old Viking ships to be content tourists per se. We owe it to ourselves and—above all—our senses to start much simpler and closer.

How about we take the time to be curious guests in our neighborhoods, cities, and even our own houses? The way a diagonal ray of sunlight hits a business card that's been sitting on the kitchen counter for weeks just might soothe us. We could make it a point to walk down a street we've never ventured down in our hometown. If we look up long enough, we might just find a blue water tower standing calmly over the shoulders of pine trees in the distance.

Travel…yes, travel somewhere, yet it needn't be remote or exotic. Without announcing it to the world and its attention-sucking members, we should walk through the glass turnstile doors of the tallest skyscraper in our area code and take an elevator. Let's not get off until we've reached the highest floor. Perhaps there is a window with an awesome panoramic view, and there we'll find some of the most overlooked yet well-crafted patterns—the rooftops and chimneys whistling smoke and their union with the sky as far as the eye can scan. Then, we should place a hand on the glass. Close our eyes. Inhale deeply. And listen to whatever sounds come. That is traveling.

A black child will play with a white child. A Mexican child will play with a Puerto Rican child. A Palestinian child will play with an Israeli child. An Indian child will play with a Pakistani child. Their adults find ways to quarrel. Let us be more childlike.

COOS BAY, OR

She said we'd visit the sand dunes in matching socks
and inhale the smell of lumber and caffeine.
If work allowed me,
she suggested we could bend the entire coast
and return less civilized.
Our flapjacks in a log cabin never happened;
I was supposed to touch Pre's Rock.
Now I'm just here,
pushing colored pins into a map,
ordering fishermen beanies online,
waiting to be captured for the weekend.
At least my bedsheets yell timber.

You know you're getting over a lost love when you can listen to the songs you used to play together by yourself and turn off the radio with a dry face.

Quick observation: Whenever someone goes to great lengths to show how amazing they look, there's a good chance they don't feel that way on the inside. There's a story behind those abs…

My deepest prayer for my children and all the children—preschool, middle-aged, and elderly—is that they discover something they feel so passionate about and dedicated to that it will cause them to rise early in the morning and stay up well into the night outlasting candlewicks. If they have yet to find that such thing, I hope they run wildly, barge through iron doors, and turn over every moss-covered boulder in desperate search until their public smiles match private expressions. Amen.

Turn on the television and it's there. Open a self-help book and the words meet our eyes promptly. Scroll through a social media post and the individual who wants to pick up the shards left in the aftermath of a broken union will poetically indoctrinate his handpicked disciples. LOVE YOURSELF…LOVE YOURSELF…LOVE YOURSELF. They all scream this. Truly, we must accept whatever "version of me" looks back at us in the mirror as we brush our teeth and condition our scalps. This includes our faults, our dreams unfulfilled, and the extra slabs of skin the body gradually invites over the years. It is a declaration that the road is under construction and that the double yellow lines are currently being drawn. However, we were not made to go through it alone; we are most certainly relational beings! From someone in our corner, we were meant to hear the words "I believe in you." We were created to enjoy the feel of holding someone's hand through a wild garden. No one wants to come home to inanimate souvenirs and mum furniture for long if they're really being honest. When wars conclude, what admirals set their compasses in the direction of vacant villages and one-man parades? No, we were assembled to make love and put it on display in the front window. Perhaps it begins with us taking off our armor while being fully aware we could be damaged forever if the lance pierces a vital artery. Is it a bet worth placing? Ultimately, loving you first will help me love me. Give us a chance.

DOG HAIR

I stepped out of the warm shower,
and put on a freezing sweatshirt that sat in a bin for months.
My winter clothes still have your mutt's hair on them.
I'd buy all new clothes,
and donate the memories for sport.
Besides, it wouldn't matter:
I'm still a two-legged dog who bathes regularly.
There's no shedding that.

A lot can be revealed about a person when a significant sum of money is given to or taken away from him. His behavior in eras of abundance as well as want is his legacy.

Children will do something to a man. They can turn the most heed-less of brutes into bread-passing diplomats or someone in between. One's unbridled default being force and hammer now seeks a grace that befalls ballerinas under scrutiny. Children—yes, the impres-sionable babes—remain the world's greatest molders of clay.

dis·ci·pline

/ˈdisˌplˌn/

a sometimes painful, occasionally anxiety-inducing, yet always meant to refine (*noun*)

the act of doing what one has to do so that one can be what one envisioned.

Be you—the rough, weathered, still-standing you. That's enough. For any calendar. Inside any stubborn margin. Across rigid state lines. Under all waving flags. You.

THE END. YES, REALLY.

ABOUT THE AUTHOR

 Born and raised in Buffalo, New York, LaGuan grew up in a big family, in which treasures like the arts, sports, and sense of community were things to be welcomed and celebrated. He holds a degree in communication from Buffalo State College and works as a letter carrier. In his spare time, he is an avid runner, reader, and, of course, dreamer. Not one who readily accepts all popular notions without doing his own bit of probing, LaGuan believes he's at his best in front of his computer with a warm cup of green tea, typing away and particularly when he's experiencing new adventures with his two children, Violet and Landry. *While Waiting* marks his first book.

CPSIA information can be obtained
at www.ICGtesting.com
Printed in the USA
LVHW091046150320
650078LV00002B/703